GUIDE TO
SOUTH KOREA

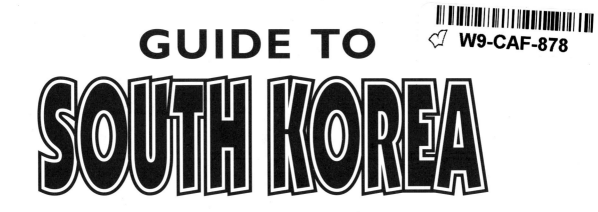

MICHAEL MARCH

Highlights for Children

CONTENTS

On the cover: Six-hundred-year-old Namdaemun Gate in the center of Seoul, South Korea

The publisher is grateful for the assistance of Min Lee in reviewing this book. Ms. Lee holds a master's degree in education from the University of Pennsylvania and a bachelor's degree in English literature from Sookmyung Women's University. She is a private instructor in Wayne, Pennsylvania, who teaches English as a second language to students in high school and college.

Published by Highlights for Children
© 1996 Highlights for Children, Inc.
P.O. Box 18201
Columbus, Ohio 43218-0201
For information on *Top Secret Adventures,* visit www.tsadventures.com or call 1-800-962-3661.

All rights reserved. No part of this book may be reproduced or transmitted in any form or by any means, electronic or mechanical, including photocopying, recording, or by any information storage and retrieval system, without permission in writing from the publisher.

10 9 8 7 6
ISBN 0-87534-924-2

EUROPE

ASIA

 South Korea

AFRICA

AUSTRALIA

ANTARCTICA

△ **South Korea's flag**
The symbols on this
flag are rich with
meaning. The circular
yin-yang (*ŭm-yang* in
Korean) suggests
balance of universal
forces. Other symbols
represent the seasons,
as well as heaven,
water, earth, and fire.

SOUTH KOREA AT A GLANCE

Area 38,300 square miles (99,390 square kilometers)

Population 48,289,037

Capital Seoul (Sŏul), population 11,000,000

Other big cities Pusan (population 3,900,000), Taegu (2,500,000)

Highest mountain on Cheju Do Island, Halla San, 6,400 feet (1,950 meters); on mainland, Jiri San, 6,320 feet (1,915 meters)

Longest river Naktong-gang, 325 miles (525 kilometers)

Largest lake Ch'ungju Lake, 255 square miles (650 square kilometers)

Official language Korean

▽ **South Korean postage stamps** Some shown here honor the country's people, flag, farming, and airline. Others show examples of South Korea's plants.

▷ **South Korean money** The Republic of Korea's currency is the *won* (₩). There are bills of ₩1,000, ₩5,000, and ₩10,000. The Korean language has words for numbers only up to 99, so bank notes are counted in Chinese numbers.

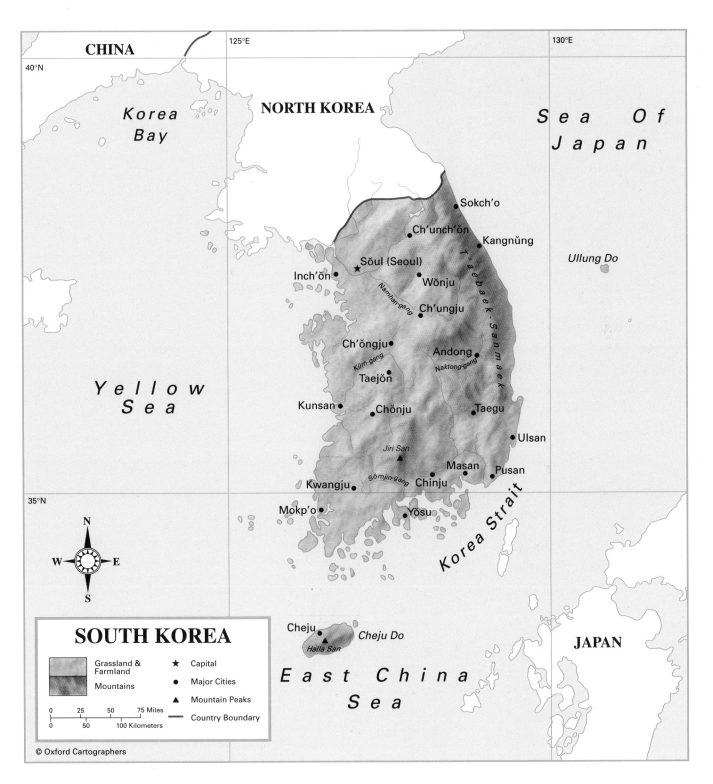

CHINA

125°E

130°E

40°N

NORTH KOREA

Korea Bay

S e a   O f   J a p a n

Sokch'o

Ch'unch'ŏn

Kangnŭng

Ullung Do

★ Sŏul (Seoul)

Wŏnju

Inch'ŏn

Namhan-gang

Ch'ungju

Ch'ŏngju

T'aebaek-Sanmaek

Andong

Kŭm-gang

Naktong-gang

Taejŏn

Y e l l o w   S e a

Kunsan

Chŏnju

Taegu

Ulsan

Jiri San ▲

Masan

Kwangju

Sŏmjin-gang

Chinju

Pusan

35°N

Mokp'o

Yŏsu

Korea Strait

N
W   E
S

SOUTH KOREA

Grassland & Farmland

Mountains

★ Capital

● Major Cities

▲ Mountain Peaks

── Country Boundary

| 0 | 25 | 50 | 75 Miles |

| 0 | 50 | | 100 Kilometers |

© Oxford Cartographers

Cheju

Cheju Do

▲ *Halla San*

E a s t   C h i n a   S e a

JAPAN

5

LAND OF THE MORNING CALM

The ancient land of Korea lies on the eastern coast of Asia. Korea is a peninsula that stretches about 600 miles (1,000 kilometers) southward into the East China Sea. It is full of beautiful forests and mountains. Its old name is Chosŏn, which means "Land of the Morning Calm."

In winter the mountain peaks are sometimes covered in snow. Fall turns the green forests into a blaze of red and gold. The warm summers bring heavy monsoon rains. These may be followed by violent storms that batter the coast and the tiny islands clustered around the mainland.

In 1948, the Korean peninsula was divided into two countries — North Korea and South Korea. The border is closed between the two countries, whose governments are still enemies. South Korea is slightly smaller in area than North Korea, but more than 45 million people live here — twice as many as in the North. As you journey through South Korea, you will find the people friendly and helpful.

The Koreans are an ancient people, with a history that goes back 5,000 years. They have their own language. Their writing, called *han'gŭl*, is quite different from Chinese.

Korea's important traditional religions are Buddhism and Confucianism. These both arrived long ago from China. Even older is Shamanism, an ancient form of spirit worship. Today, many South Koreans are Christians.

South Korea is a fascinating mix of the old and the new. The people still plant rice for their main food, as they have done for thousands of years. But their factories produce the latest models of cars and computers, which are sold all around the world. And on festival days every South Korean enjoys dressing up in the *hanbok*, the traditional costume.

▷ **Korean Exhibition Center building** The modern skyscraper towers above Seoul, South Korea's capital.

▽ **Growing rice** Seeds are sown in flooded fields and the shoots are replanted.

▽ **A religious ceremony** Men in traditional robes at Chongmyo shrine in Seoul honor the memory of Korea's ancient kings.

CAPITAL CITY

The heart of South Korea is its capital Seoul (Sŏul) in the northwestern part of the country. It is a beautiful city built across hills and valleys. For over 500 years Seoul was the capital of the old Korean kingdom of Chosŏn. Later, in 1948, South Korea became a republic with Seoul as its capital. Today it is a busy city with eleven million people.

▽ **A Seoul boulevard** Most buildings have signs in English as well as Korean.

In the center of Seoul there is a bronze statue of a great Korean hero, Admiral Yi Sun-shin. He is famous for his victories over the Japanese in sea battles 400 years ago. South of here, Namdaemun Gate is one of Korea's oldest wooden buildings. It was built in 1398 and marked the southern entrance to the city. It has been restored and is now surrounded by office buildings and roads.

Nearby, you can explore the crowded alleys of the city's oldest market. Here you can buy almost anything, from fish and flowers to ginseng, the famous herb that is used as a medicine. You will also find silk shirts and the beautiful blue-green celadon pottery. Often there is no fixed price and you have to bargain with the storekeeper.

Seoul is a shopper's paradise. At one of Asia's biggest electronics markets, you can find an inexpensive computer. In Myŏng-dong district you can buy fashionable clothes. Buses or subway trains will take you where you want to go all around the city.

There are thousands of restaurants in Seoul. Most of them serve delicious local dishes such as *kalbi-tchim*, a rich stew made of beef ribs. Some restaurants have their own theater, where you can watch graceful Korean dancing as you enjoy your meal.

▷ **Mount Nam, Seoul** At the top, Seoul Tower is 1,575 feet (480 meters) high. From here you get a marvelous view over the city.

◁ **A shopper's paradise** Stores in Seoul offer goods from clothing to computers. Here, customers look for bargains at an outdoor stall.

PALACES AND SKYSCRAPERS

The ancient kings who made Seoul their capital also built the lovely Kyŏngbokkung Palace. This was not just one construction but many buildings with their own grounds surrounded by a high wall. Korean kings lived here in splendor for nearly 200 years. Then in 1592 Japanese troops invaded Korea and burned the buildings to the ground. Today some of the finest parts of the palace have been restored to their former glory.

The main gate of Kyŏngbokkung Palace is a magnificent pavilion with three arches. Nearby, mythical animals symbolize justice. Pass through here and you come to the huge wooden Throne Hall with its elegant red-and-blue painted ceiling. This is where Korean kings were once crowned. Outside in the courtyard stands a marble pagoda, or tower, that is ten stories high. It is even older than the palace itself.

△ **Seoul's Olympic Stadium** This shows the opening ceremonies of the Olympic Games.

▷ **The gardens of Kyŏngbokkung Palace** Shrubs are in bloom.

Not far away is another royal palace, where members of the royal family lived until 1990. Behind it there is a 78-acre (32-hectare) park with thousand-year-old trees. The park is known as the Secret Garden. It is dotted with pavilions, and its streams and ponds feature lovely bridges. Women of the royal court used to go to the park to be alone.

Seoul lies on the Han-gang River. On the south bank you see the great Olympic stadium, where the 1988 Olympic Games were held. From the nearby ferry port double-decker riverboats sail downstream to Yŏŭido Island. From the river you get a good view of the city and the spires of some of Seoul's churches. Yŏŭido Island is known as "Seoul's Manhattan" because of its many skyscrapers. A huge domed building on the island houses the Korean parliament. Its assembly hall is said to be the biggest in Asia.

△ **City Hall Plaza in the center of Seoul**
Buses, taxis, and subway trains stop here.

11

WALLS AND FRONTIERS

Southeast of Seoul, the mountain Namhan San is a popular place for a picnic. Here you can breathe fresh mountain air and look down on the Han-gang valley below. A wall winds across the top of the mountain. It was built 2,000 years ago to keep out invaders. Later it was strengthened.

One of Korea's most famous kings was King Sejong, who ruled from 1418 to 1450. He invented *han'gŭl*, the Korean alphabet. Until that time, Korean was written using Chinese characters. You can visit King Sejong's tomb close to the town of Yŏju.

A marble monument with an inscription in han'gŭl stands in front of the burial mound.

In 1636 an army from Manchuria, the region to the north of Korea, broke through the wall on Namhan San and conquered the Korean kingdom. From 1650 Korea shut itself off from the rest of the world. For over 200 years its only contact with foreigners was through the ports of Inch'ŏn and Pusan.

An expressway leads from Yŏju, past the old town of Suwon, to Inch'ŏn, a big port. The trip by car, across open country, takes about an hour and a half.

◁ **A Korean potter** Celadon stoneware has been made in Korea for more than a thousand years. Celadon is pottery famous for its blue-green glaze. Korean potters also have a long tradition of making the fine, hard pottery called porcelain.

▷ **Straw-thatched houses in the Korean Folk Village, near Suwon** People live and work here much as they did long ago. Blacksmiths, silk-weavers, farmers, basket-makers, and fortune-tellers are all part of this colorful, living museum.

▷ **Moment of victory at a school sports day** Children, teachers, and parents all take part in the final game of the day.

Today, South Korea has little contact with its neighbor North Korea. More than fifty years ago the two countries were at war with each other. The village of P'anmunjŏm lies in a narrow strip of land between the North and South Korean borders. North and South Korean troops face each other across this "no-man's-land." In P'anmunjŏm you can visit the conference room where, in 1953, the Armistice Agreement was signed, ending the war. If you stand next to the North Korean flag, at the far end of the conference table, you are in North Korea.

RELIGIOUS TRADITIONS

Taegu lies on the route linking Seoul with Korea's southeast coast. It is a big industrial city known for its cloth and its traditional markets. But Taegu is most famous for growing tasty apples. Most of South Korea's apples grow in the vast orchards around Taegu. The city is surrounded by mountains more than 3,500 feet (1,100 meters) high. It is said to have both the coldest and the hottest weather of all South Korean cities.

A two-hour drive from the center of the city past high cliffs and tumbling streams brings you to one of the country's finest temples. Haeinsa Temple sits in the mountains, surrounded by misty forest. From time to time the silence here is broken by the chanting of the Buddhist monks. The Buddhist religion came to Korea through China from India. Haeinsa Temple's many treasures include the 80,000 sacred printing blocks called the *Tripitaka Koreana*. The wooden blocks are carved on both sides with Buddhist scriptures written in Chinese characters. Work on the blocks began in 1236, during an invasion by the Mongols. It took fifteen years to complete.

▽ **A Korean dinner for special occasions** This meal usually includes salted fish, two kinds of soup, rice, and about ten other dishes, which vary from region to region.

▷ **Fishing boats on Ullŭngdo Island** The catch is mainly squid. The freshly caught fish are stored in baskets until the fishing boats return to port.

Farther north, near the ancient town of Andong, you can see an enormous figure of Buddha carved into the rock. Buses go from Andong to Hahoe, an old village on the Naktong-gang River. Here, at festival time, the villagers perform lively dances wearing brightly painted masks.

P'ohang, on the east coast, is South Korea's great steelmaking town. From the harbor, you can take a hydrofoil, a fast boat, to the beautiful volcanic island of Ullŭng Do in the stormy Sea of Japan. Fishing is the main activity of people living on the island.

▽ **Traditional clothes** This woman is dressed in the costume typically worn by ladies of royalty in eighteenth-century South Korea.

THE OPEN-AIR MUSEUM

Shilla was the strongest of three Korean kingdoms that arose 2,000 years ago. Its capital was Kyŏngju, east of Taegu. Kyŏngju is a city so full of historic monuments that it is called "the museum without walls." For nearly 250 years the Shilla kings ruled all of the Korean peninsula. One of Shilla's great heroes was General Kim Yu Sin. His tomb sits on a hill overlooking Kyŏngju. Legend tells how the first Korean to be named Kim was Kim Al-chi, an early Shilla king. Today, one in five Korean families is called Kim.

Many of Shilla's kings are buried in and around Kyŏngju. You can see gold crowns and other treasures discovered in their tombs at the city's museum. There, too, you will find one of the world's biggest bells. The great bronze Emille Bell was cast more than 1,200 years ago. Long ago, when the bell was sounded, it could be heard 25 miles (40 kilometers) away.

Even older than the Emille Bell is Kyŏngju's ancient observatory. This bottle-shaped tower is made up of 366 stones and stands 30 feet (9 meters) high.

▷ **A "guardian king of Heaven," Pulguksa temple** He is one of the fierce-looking figures found at the entrance to Korean Buddhist temples.

Just outside Kyŏngju is Pulguksa, one of Korea's most famous Buddhist temples. Its many wooden buildings stand above one another on terraces linked by long stone stairways. Seen from above, the temple roofs look like a beautiful rolling sea of tiles.

A long road winds uphill from the temple to Mount Tóham. Here, in a grotto, a statue of Buddha sits gazing out across the Sea of Japan. The beautiful figure is made from a single piece of white granite. When the sun rises in the morning, it lights up the statue's face.

◁ **The marina at Pomun Lake outside Kyŏngju**
Pomun is a large tourist center with hotels, shops, restaurants, tennis courts, a golf course, an open-air theater, and a beautiful lake. "Swan boats," like this one, cruise the lake.

▷ **Tumuli Park, Kyŏngju**
The mounds are the burial places of more than twenty Shilla kings and members of their families.

ON THE WATERFRONT

Pusan lies in a valley surrounded by mountains on South Korea's southeast coast. Nearly four million people live in Pusan. It is South Korea's second-largest city. From the top of Pusan Tower, you get a good view of the city and the harbor below. Long, sandy beaches and the mild climate bring tourists here. Some also come to bathe in the hot springs, which are said to cure diseases. Others watch the thousands of migrating birds that feed at the mouth of the Naktong River.

High on a mountain above the city, you can explore the country's largest fortress. Its great walls are 10.5 miles (17 kilometers) long. The fortress is guarded on all sides by four huge gates built in traditional Korean style.

Down on the waterfront, ships' cargoes are unloaded at the wharf or loaded up to be shipped abroad. Pusan is the country's biggest seaport. Many of the materials needed by South Korea's car-making plants and shipyards are brought in by ship from foreign countries. More ships are built in South Korea than in any other country in the world except Japan.

West of Pusan's Yŏngdo Bridge you will find the huge fish market. Early in the morning the fishing fleets unload their catches in big baskets onto the wharf. Watch buyers haggling with the fishermen over the prices they charge. In the crowded fish market halls, you can have a tasty snack of fresh lobster or raw fish with green horseradish and garlic.

For an overnight stop, stay at a *yŏgwan*, a Korean inn. Many of Pusan's yŏgwans are near the bus and railroad stations. Your room is small, with sliding paper walls. You take off your shoes before entering. The bedding includes a mattress, which you unroll onto the floor, a quilt, and a hard pillow stuffed with wheat husks. In winter an underfloor heating system, called *ondol*, keeps the room warm.

▷ **A Korean craftsman at work** He is making brushes for artists. Korean calligraphy is the art of using brushes and ink to write *han'gŭl*.

▽ **Cars for export** Ulsan is an industrial town north of Pusan. One of South Korea's biggest companies, Hyundai, is located here. Hyundai manufactures automobiles and ships, as well as electronic goods.

▽ **Cherry blossoms on the streets of Chinhae** The naval port of Chinhae lies west of Pusan. The city's streets are lined with cherry trees, which bloom in April.

CRATER ISLAND

Around South Korea's shores there are more than 3,000 islands. The largest of these is Cheju Do, which lies 60 miles (100 kilometers) off the southwest coast. From Pusan, the ferry takes twelve hours to make the crossing. The people of Cheju Do speak a Korean dialect that dates back 700 years to the Mongol invasion. The Mongols also taught the islanders to breed horses, and today Cheju Do's ponies are famous.

In the middle of the island sits the beautiful Halla San, South Korea's highest mountain. Its snowcapped peak rises to 6,400 feet (1,950 meters) and can be seen from all over the island. To climb to the top takes at least two and a half hours. You will need hiking boots, a warm sweater, and a parka to keep off the rain. The weather on the mountain can change suddenly.

The mountain is an extinct volcano. The craters, lava tunnels, caves, and strangely shaped rocks that you see on the island were made by volcanic eruptions long ago. You will also find waterfalls and forests on Cheju Do, as well as sandy beaches, orange groves, and yellow rapeseed fields.

The island's traditional houses are built of black lava rock. So are many of the *Tolharubang*, ancient "grandfather" sculptures, that have bulging eyes and huge noses. These statues are among the island's most famous sights. People once believed that they protected the island.

For hundreds of years Cheju Do has been famous for its women divers. Deep down on the sea bed they look for oysters, mussels, cuttlefish, sea cucumbers, sea urchins, and seaweed. The divers can hold their breath underwater for four minutes. Today they wear rubber wet suits and masks rather than the traditional cotton costume.

▽ **A market stall on Cheju Do Island** At the front is ginseng root. Koreans have used this plant as a medicine for thousands of years.

▷ **Crater lake on Halla San** There are many volcanic craters on Cheju Do. They have been formed by eruptions thousands of years ago.

▷ **Cheju City harbor** Cheju City is Cheju Do Island's biggest town. It lies on the northern shore and has an international airport.

SOUTH BY SOUTHWEST

You can fly from Cheju Do to Yŏsu, a port on the south coast of the mainland. Between here and Pusan to the east, the rocky coast twists and turns, and the sea is dotted with hundreds of beautiful islands.

It was in these waters, four hundred years ago, that Admiral Yi Sun-shin's "turtle ships" won great sea battles against much bigger Japanese fleets. The islands are rich in history. You can see a full-size copy of a turtle ship, with its iron armor, on Tolsan Do Island. A number of the turtle ships were built on the island of Namhae Do. Today, one of the biggest suspension bridges in all East Asia crosses from Namhae Do to the mainland. The hard, straight bamboo that grows on Odong Do Island was used by Admiral Yi's archers to make their arrows.

The southwest of South Korea is less hilly than the rest of the country. Here, on the Honam Plain, you can see long stretches of rice paddies. Nearby, the city of Kwangju is famous for rice wine. Watermelon fields and tea plantations overlook the city from Mount Mudŭng. The tea is grown by Buddhist monks. They pick the buds early in the year, just after the snows. This "spring tea" is good for both the body and the mind.

Farther north is Chŏnju, known as "paper city." The finest paper in Asia comes from here. You can buy beautiful paper fans, oiled paper umbrellas, and finely textured art paper. The paper, called *hanji*, is mostly made from mulberry trees. Some of it is still made and dyed by hand in traditional ways. You can often see big, freshly made paper sheets hanging out to dry, like laundry.

Chŏnju is also famous for its food. Try the local dish *pibimpap*, a delicious mixture of rice, raw ground beef, and fresh greens in a spicy sauce.

◁ **Working with bamboo** Tamyang, a town near Kwangju, is the Korean center for bamboo crafts. Bamboo baskets, spoons, furniture, and other items are made here.

▷ **Mount Mai, east of Chŏnju** The mountain's shape gives it its name — Mai San means "Horse Ears Mount." Between the two peaks there is a pagoda temple built of rocks.

▽ **Farming on the Honam Plain** This region is known as the "rice bin of Korea." Wheat and vegetables such as carrots and cabbage are also grown here.

HISTORIC PLACES

For a few weeks in the summer of 1950, the capital of South Korea was Taejŏn. The government moved here when Seoul was attacked by North Korean troops at the start of the Korean War. Taejŏn was itself later attacked and damaged. Today much of the city is rebuilt. Outside the modern city you will find a science park with futuristic buildings and an exciting roller coaster.

Two historic towns lie to the west of Taejŏn. Kongju and, later, Puyŏ were the capitals of the ancient Paekche kingdom. The kingdom lasted nearly seven hundred years. At its greatest, it stretched across western and central Korea. The end came in the year 660, when Puyŏ fell to the armies of the Shilla kingdom in the south. On a hill above the town, you can see the remains of the fortress where the Paekche armies made their last stand. Every October, the people of Kongju take part in a festival to celebrate the town's Paekche origins. They hold street parades, set off firecrackers, and dance on the sandy banks of the Kŭm-gang River.

The Ŭnjin Miruk is the tallest stone statue of Buddha in the country. It is 59 feet (18 meters) high. It is also one of the most unusual statues. The head, hands, and enormous crown all look too large for the body. The statue stands in the grounds of a temple called Candlelight Temple, outside the town of Nonsan. Both the temple and the statue are over a thousand years old.

▽ **Independence Hall, Ch'ŏnan, northwest of Taejŏn** The towers represent the South Koreans' hopes for union with North Korea.

◁ **Korean fan maker**
Making fans is an art that has been practiced for hundreds of years in Korea. Fans are often used in traditional dances.

▽ **Pŏpchusa Temple, northeast of Taejŏn** The huge brass statue of Buddha in the courtyard stands 108 feet (33 meters) high.

LAKES AND MOUNTAINS

Buses leave Taejŏn for Ch'unch'ŏn, in the northeast, four times a day. Ch'unch'ŏn is a pretty town at the center of the lake district. Soyangho Lake, to the east, is the biggest man-made lake in South Korea. It was formed when the Soyang Dam was built. Ferries go up and down the lake, or you can explore its blue waters by speedboat. In summer the water level is lowered before the coming of the monsoon rains.

Ch'unch'ŏn is known for its silk. Here you can visit a factory where silk is made in the traditional way. Silk is spun from cocoons of silkworms. The cocoons are soaked in boiling water to free the silken yarn. Silkworms develop from the caterpillars of the silk moth. They feed on the leaves of mulberry trees, which grow around the town.

On the northeast coast you can enjoy white sandy beaches and dine on freshly caught fish. South of the big fishing port of Sokch'o, a temple overlooks the sea from high up on a cliff surrounded by pine forest. A huge white statue of Kwanum, the Goddess of Mercy, looks out from it. Local families pray to the goddess for the safety of their fishermen at sea.

Buses from Sokch'o go to Mt. Sŏrak National Park. Sŏrak San means "Snow Peak Mountain." Here you can explore some of the finest scenery in the country, hiking through forest and up mountain trails. You can walk across swaying bridges slung high over steep gorges. There are wonderful views. You can also discover old temples and castles hidden deep in the mountains and forests. In the northeast, and all over South Korea, there are always beautiful things to see and exciting things to do.

▷ **Kŭm-gang waterfall, Mount Sŏrak National Park** This is one of many beautiful waterfalls in the park. In autumn the trees are full of reds and golds.

▽ **Yongpeong (Dragon Valley)** This ski resort has ski slopes with chair lifts and snow-making machines.

▽ **Hiking on Sŏrak San** People come all year round to enjoy the mountain park.

SOUTH KOREA FACTS AND FIGURES

People

Most people in South (and North) Korea belong to a single ethnic group. They are descended from the Mongols and Manchus of northern, eastern, and central Asia. There are also a few ethnic Chinese living in South Korea.

Trade and Industry

South Korea makes a wide variety of goods for sale at home and abroad. Clothing and shoes made in South Korea are sold all over the world. So too are chemicals, machinery, ships, and cars, as well as electronic goods, such as computers and televisions. South Korea also has large steelmaking plants and oil refineries. However, the country has few mineral resources of its own, except for a little coal and iron ore. All its oil and most of its metal ores are brought in from other countries.

Most of the country's electricity is from oil-burning power stations. But there are some hydroelectric power stations on the Han-gang River. Ten big companies, including car makers Hyundai and Daewoo and electronics producer Samsung (the three biggest), own nearly a third of South Korea's factories.

△ **Noltwigi (Korean see-saw)** Women dressed in colorful *hanbok* send each other flying into the air.

Farming

Because South Korea is mostly mountainous, only about one-fifth of the land can be farmed. Some farmers also catch fish.

Rice is the main crop. It is grown mostly in the south and west. Farmers also grow corn, soybeans, cabbage, carrots, onions, and other vegetables. They also grow apples and pears, and other edible plants, such as ginger and garlic. Pigs and cattle are kept for their meat, and chickens provide both meat and eggs.

Mulberry trees, for feeding silkworms, are important plants. So too are tobacco and ginseng.

Laver and oysters are farmed in large scale.

Fishing

Fish is a major part of the South Korean diet. There are large fishing fleets at ports such as Pusan, Mokpo, and Sokch'o. Small fishing villages are dotted all along the coasts. Sea bream, flatfish, sea squirt, squid, and octopus are a few of the fish that are caught. Some of the fish is sold abroad.

There are also fish farms, where fish are specially raised for food.

Food

Korean food is both tasty and healthy. It often includes garlic. Soup and rice are usually served with every meal. Here are some delicious Korean dishes:
kimch'i: salted cabbage or other vegetables pickled in spices (Some kimch'i include octopus, shrimp, pear, chestnuts, or oysters.)
pulgogi: strips of barbecued beef or pork that have been soaked in a mixture of rice wine, sesame seed oil, garlic, sugar, and soy sauce
samgyet'ang: stewed chicken stuffed with ginseng, rice, and garlic, and served in a clay pot
chŏnbokchuk (abalone porridge): abalone slices fried in sesame oil, then cooked with rice and water

Schools

All children over the age of six spend six years at primary school. Most children then attend middle school for another three years, learning to read, write, and speak English or another foreign language.

Middle school is followed by three more years at high school. After that, many high school students go on to study at a university or college of higher education.

△ **Dancers wearing traditional masks**
The village of Hahoe, near Andong, is famous for its masked dances.

Literature

The first known Korean writing was a poem composed about 2,000 years ago. Most early prose told about history or religion. *Tripitaka Koreana* was included in the Cultural Heritage List in 1997 by UNESCO for its technology in printing and preservation.

Today, Korean authors such as Yi Kwangsu, Park Kyŏngnī, and poet So Jongju are world famous.

The Media

About forty daily newspapers are published in South Korea. Two of them, the *Korea Herald* and *Korea Times*, appear in English. More than 800 weekly or monthly magazines cover all topics from sports and fashion to politics. The *Korea Post*, a monthly general-interest magazine, is in English.

There are four national and thirty cable television networks, which broadcast in Korean. These show a mixture of educational programs, sports, movies, and news. There are also eight national radio stations and many local ones. A radio and television network is run by Americans for U.S. military personnel based in South Korea.

Music and Drama

More than forty traditional Korean instruments are still played today. They include the *changgo* (an hourglass-shaped drum), *taegŭm* (a long bamboo flute), and *kayagŭm* (a 12-stringed zither).

Music accompanies traditional drama and dance. Many dances are very old. Some belong to the times of the Korean kings and their courts. The liveliest dances are the folk dances such as the "farmers' dance." The dancers spin around to a rhythm beaten out by drums and gongs. In *p'ansori*, a dramatic song, a singer tells a sad story to the accompaniment of a drumbeat. *Ch'ang* musical dramas are like Western operas.

Art

Koreans have been making pottery for about 5,000 years. They are best known for their beautiful celadon and porcelain ware.

Traditional Korean painting is done on paper or silk. It shows landscapes with birds, trees, flowers, waterfalls, or houses.

Many of the bronze or stone Buddha figures in South Korea's temples are fine examples of Korean sculpture. The temple buildings have graceful, long, curved roofs turned up at the edges and covered in tiles. Beautiful gold-winged crowns and jewelry made of gold and jade have been found in many of the tombs of Korean kings.

SOUTH KOREA FACTS AND FIGURES

Religion

The oldest Korean religion is Shamanism. Buddhism came to Korea from China about 1,600 years ago. Korea's main religion since the 1100s is based on Confucianism. Confucius taught people to respect their rulers and others and not make war.

Christianity came to Korea much later. Today about 20 percent of South Koreans are Christian.

Sports

All kinds of sports are enjoyed in South Korea. Western sports, such as baseball and soccer, are popular. So too are traditional sports like *tae kwondo*. This is an ancient form of self-defense in which players strike each other with their fists and feet. *Ssirŭm*, Korean wrestling, also has a big following. The aim of Ssirŭm is for each participant to try to throw the opponent onto the floor.

Historically, Koreans have been known for their skill at archery, and today this is a popular national sport. Other sports are hiking and climbing, skiing, swimming, and fishing. Tennis and golf are popular with both players and spectators.

△ **White herons** South Korea is home to about 380 species of birds. Some species, including the white heron, are now protected by law.

Festivals

South Koreans love to dress up for their many festivals, which often have no fixed dates.

April **Cherry Blossom Festival** Held at Chinhae in honor of Korea's hero Admiral Yi Sun-shin

April or May **Buddha's Birthday** Lanterns are hung in the temples and there are lantern parades.

June **Andong Folk Festival** People perform masked dances and engage in a chariot game called Ch'ajŏn Nori

September or October **Ch' usok** (Korean Thanksgiving) Time to visit ancestors' graves

Plants

The Korean peninsula is rich in plant life. Pine and fir trees and alpine flowers grow in the colder north. Oak, beech, cedar, and larch trees are also found here and farther south. Rhododendrons flower throughout the peninsula, but are most plentiful in the north. Beautiful forsythia thrives in the central region along with pine, hazel, chestnut rowan, ash, and lime trees. The south has colorful camellias, heathers, and ancient ginkgo trees.

Animals

The Korean tiger is now extinct. But many different kinds of animals and birds still have a home on the Korean peninsula. Brown and black bears and deer roam the forests and mountains, which are also home to woodpeckers and hawk owls. Some bird species, such as the ibis, white stork, black stork, and black vulture, are now protected, as is the rare red-crested Manchurian crane. Bears are also protected, along with the *Chindo-kae*, a short-haired dog that comes from Chindo Island off the southwest coast.

HISTORY

Tribespeople from northern and central Asia came to the Korean peninsula about 30,000 years ago. According to legend, the first Korean king was Tangun, who came to the throne in 2333 B.C. and ruled for 1,500 years. He built his capital at Pyŏngyang (now the capital of North Korea). In 108 B.C. northern Korea came under the rule of China. But later that century, three Korean kingdoms arose and the Chinese were driven out. In the 7th century A.D. the Shilla kingdom, by far the strongest of the three, defeated its rivals with China's help and unified the country. This was the beginning of a "golden age" of Korean culture.

From 1231-1270, Korea was invaded by and under the influence of Mongols from the north. About 400 years later, the Manchu rulers of China also invaded Korea. The Koreans then closed their country to the rest of the world for more than 200 years. They eventually began to trade with the U.S. and Japan. In 1910 Korea came under Japanese rule. But the Japanese withdrew from the country in 1945, at the end of World War II.

Korea divided into North and South in 1948. North Korea was supported by China and the former U.S.S.R. The U.S. backed South Korea. South Korea's first president was Syngman Rhee.

In 1950 North Korea attacked the South in an attempt to unify both countries. The war that followed lasted three years. Since then, South Korea has grown into one of Asia's most important industrial countries.

LANGUAGE

Korean belongs to the family of languages that includes Turkish, Finnish, and Mongolian. Korean is spoken throughout both North and South Korea. The written language uses a simple alphabet called *han'gŭl*. It has twenty-four letters. Letters are written above and below one another as well as side by side. Han'gŭl was invented more than 500 years ago. Before then, Korean was written with Chinese characters. Korean words can be written in English with marks to show pronunciation.

Useful words and phrases

English	Korean
Zero	*yong*
One	*il*
Two	*ee*
Three	*sam*
Four	*sa*
Five	*o*
Six	*yuk*
Seven	*ch'il*
Eight	*p'al*
Nine	*ku*
Ten	*ship*
Sunday	*īryoīl*
Monday	*woryoīl*
Tuesday	*hwayoil*

Useful words and phrases

English	Korean
Wednesday	*suyoil*
Thursday	*mokyoil*
Friday	*kŭmyoil*
Saturday	*t'oyoil*
Hello	*Annyong haseyo*
Good morning	*Annyong haseyo*
Good night	*Annyonghi jumushipshiyo*
Good-bye	*Annyonghi gaseyo*
Please	*Put'ak hamnida*
Thank you	*Kamsa hamnida*
How do you do?	*Ch'ŏŭm poepgessŭmnida?*

INDEX

Acknowledgments
Book created for Highlights for Children, Inc. by Bender Richardson White.
Editors: Peter MacDonald and Lionel Bender
Designer: Malcolm Smythe
Art Editor: Ben White
Editorial Assistant: Madeleine Samuel
Picture Researcher: Madeleine Samuel
Production: Kim Richardson

Maps produced by Oxford Cartographers, England.
Banknotes from Thomas Cook Currency Services.
Stamps from Stanley Gibbons.

Editorial Consultant: Andrew Gutelle
Guide to South Korea is approved by the Korea National Tourism Organization, London
Managing Editor, Highlights New Products: Margie Hayes Richmond

Picture credits
EU = Eye Ubiquitous. KNTC = Korea National Tourism Corporation, London. Z = Zefa. t= top, b= bottom, r = right, l = left. Cover: Z. Pages: 6t, 6b: KNTC. 7r: Z/Damm. 8: Piet Opperman. 9t: Art Directors & Trip. 9b: Korean Overseas Culture and Information Service. 10l: EU. 10-11: Viesti Associates. 11r: Korea National Tourism Organization. 12, 13t, 13b: KNTC. 14l, 14-15, 15r: KNTC. 16, 17b: KNTC. 17t: EU/L. Fordyce. 18-19, 19tl, 19tr: KNTC. 20, 21t: EU/L. Fordyce. 21b: EU. 22, 23t, 23b: KNTC. 24, 25t, 25b: KNTC. 26-27, 27b: EU. 27t: KNTC. 28, 29, 30: KNTC.
Illustration on page 1 by Tom Powers.